City Gardens

Creative Ideas for Small Spaces

Pierre Nessmann
Brigitte & Philippe Perdereau

Stewart, Tabori & Chang
New York

Published in 2008 by Stewart, Tabori & Chang
An imprint of Harry N. Abrams, Inc.

Library of Congress Cataloging-in-Publication Data

Nessmann, Pierre.
 City gardens : creative ideas for small spaces / by Pierre Nessmann ;
 photography by Brigitte and Philippe Perdereau.
    p. cm.
Includes bibliographical references and index.
ISBN 13: 978-1-58479-645-9
ISBN 10: 1-58479-645-6
1. Urban gardens. 2. Urban gardening. I. Perdereau, Brigitte. II. Perdereau, Philippe. III. Title.
SB453.N454 2008
712'.6091732—dc22
                      2007033528

Translated by Krister Swartz

Project Manager, English-language edition: Magali Veillon
Editor, English-language edition: Miranda Ottewell
Designer, English-language edition: Shawn Dahl
Production Manager, English-language edition: Tina Cameron

The text of this book was composed in Profile.

Printed and bound in France by Pollina - L 44629
10 9 8 7 6 5 4 3 2 1

HNA ▮▮▮▮▮
harry n. abrams, inc.
a subsidiary of La Martinière Groupe

115 West 18th Street
New York, NY 10011
www.hnabooks.com

CONTENTS

Tucked away in the heart of the city, small sanctuaries of greenery lie hidden behind walls and between the bulky forms of massive apartment buildings. It would seem that these towering city buildings could provide the perfect shelter for an intimate urban garden, but in fact, a somewhat harsh environment surrounds these precious spaces, which attempt to create a comfortable extension of their cultivators' living space, wrested against great odds from the world of concrete around them. The lack of sunlight, the confined atmosphere, the air pollution and noise of the city, and even the ever-present eyes of curious neighbors all conspire to create living conditions as difficult for those who work to create and use these secret gardens as for the plants that live in them. And yet, many a small city courtyard and garden still manages to be both a pleasant place to live and filled with a variety of healthy plants. A cramped space is turned into an asset, and the lack of distant views, in a setting where city walls take the place of restful glimpses of horizon, gives birth to numerous design techniques that bring perspective and interest into the garden. From a carefully planned layout to deft division of a space, from the judicious choice of plants to the selection of attractive paving materials, the principles of design and the use of a few handy tricks all help to push the boundaries of these gardens, making them appear far more spacious than they really are. ■

Imagination and Design

✳ Patios, courtyards, and small gardens in the city occupy a special place in the world of garden design. Their cramped space, which makes them all the more difficult to work out a design for, is what also gives them their charm. Their small size and odd shapes, surrounded as they often are by buildings and enclosed by walls, work together in giving them their intimate character. This rare and precious space must be used to its utmost; areas for living, such as a quiet seating nook or a play area, must share the garden with beds prepared for plants. For the best chance of creating a design that works, begin by consulting books on urban gardening in order to familiarize yourself with the plants and materials specific to this type of garden. Gather these ideas together and use them to help you come up with the layout of your dreams, and then sketch it out on a piece of paper before starting. This intermediate step of getting your garden design down on paper not only helps you better organize the space but also encourages you to evaluate the impact of choosing this or that plant down to the last detail. At the end of the day, after all, it is often difficult to rectify a mistake once your garden project has been completed. ■

The Small Urban Garden: A World of Its Own

✷ **Making an asset of cramped space.** Gardeners and landscape artists will approach small areas in different ways. To the gardener, a few dozen square yards of earth justify the name of garden, whereas the landscape artist is an habitué of parks and other grand landscapes. Still, one thing is clear: Lack of space does not have to be a handicap, and anyone who applies himself, with the aid of various techniques and a number of tricks, to creating an urban garden, however small it might be, can create a convivial and pleasant space for living. ■

1

2

3

The Town Garden

In the urban environment, where space is precious and rare, any little parcel of earth under an open sky can be considered a garden. In a large city, a few square yards of paved terrace or courtyard may be the only garden space available; a town garden, on the other hand, may be relatively spacious, even allowing the luxury of a small lawn. Even in these more generous conditions, however, the nature of the urban environment imposes restrictions on the kind of plants that can be cultivated.

A town garden generally occupies a square or rectangular plot, situated at the heart of a group of buildings and enclosing walls. The proximity of these walls considerably reduces the amount of sunlight available, so that the main requirement limiting the choice of plants for a city garden is shade tolerance. To these problems are often added soil that is of poor quality when it exists at all, the presence of intrusive tree roots, and air pollution. But the great pleasure derived from a little plot of earth in an urban area motivates its owners even more to create the most pleasant place possible, however cramped the space may be. ■

The Row House Garden

A common outcome of urban row house development is land parcels cut up into long, narrow sections. A house, which generally occupies the entire width of this plot of land, is built at the end of the lot closest to the street. The garden, then, is either found entirely behind the house or divided into two parts, usually a very small plot in the front of the house and a larger space behind it. The area in front of the house becomes a housefront or street garden, just enough to decorate the house's entryway. The area behind the house is larger, but it can only be reached by passing through the house. This is a great inconvenience when you are trying to bring in plants and other materials while creating your garden, but on the other hand, it has the advantage of insulating the finished garden from the bustle and noise of the street. Another factor to consider is that this narrow parcel behind a city row house is only one of a number of parallel strips of land, all the same shape and size, which together can create a feeling of greater space.

The long, narrow shape of the row house garden often limits its layout to a central walkway with beds on each side. If the garden is wide enough, however, it may be possible to create a succession of distinct zones, much like rooms in a house, that can divide the whole into several areas. Those closer to the house are best used as dining nooks, reading corners, or places to sit and relax. The zones farther afield are for playing and gardening. A central ribbon of lawn may connect these distinct spaces, perhaps accompanied by a walkway or flagstone path. ■

1, 2, & 3. Row house gardens cannot escape from the universal layout of a central walkway with beds for plants on either side. This shape, however, allows the designer to create an exaggerated sense of perspective, amplifying the effect of depth to give these cramped places a more spacious feeling.

1

2

3

Courtyards and Patios

4. Truly an open-air living room, this patio benefits from a sheltered micro-climate that makes it a comfortable spot from early spring all the way through to late autumn.

City courtyards are often thought of as un-attractive waste spaces where the lack of sunlight and the absence of soil make it practically impossible for plants to grow. This is also true of patios, whose name at least carries the echoes of a more glam-orous past, evoking as it does southern architecture, the sun, and an atmosphere of vacation. In fact, we would have to go back to antiquity to find the original courtyard, the open-air space nestled in the heart of Roman villas and known as the atrium. De-pending on the time of day, the atrium, whether inundated with light or ▪ ▪ ▪

...

protected from the heat of the sun, was built around a pool that was fed by rainwater running off the roofs around it. This water reserve was used to supply household needs as well as to water plants cultivated in terra-cotta pots. With the passing of centuries, the atrium has evolved to become the patio, spread far beyond the area around the Mediterranean, and integrated itself into the architecture of town and city houses everywhere. This type of garden, combining the pleasure of outdoor living with the pastime of gardening, has become a hallmark of today's lifestyle.

As the patio, deck, or courtyard is often directly connected to a main room of the house, its floor should be at the same level as the floor of the room it adjoins. This will not only enlarge your interior living space in real terms, by making it easier to pass from the interior to the exterior, but will also psychologically extend the feeling of shelter as the division of interior and exterior becomes blurred.

Since it is a sheltered area with comfortable outdoor furniture, the patio is a space that we take advantage of in every season, because of its accessibility and proximity to the house. But it is still first and foremost a garden, and thus a place to grow plants. Its sheltered setting, nestled against the house, gives it the benefit of radiant heat from the walls and protection from wind and harsh weather. This privileged situation makes it easier to grow a vast assortment of plants here, notably those from the Mediterranean area. This is one of the principal assets of the patio: Besides creating an additional room and an inviting escape, it provides a unique gardening microclimate. ■

1

Tips

Choose a material for the patio's floor that is both attractive to look at and pleasant underfoot. Wooden decking boards, for example, are easy to install, comfortable to walk on, and have a nice warm look. Their natural resistance to moisture can be reinforced with a special treatment that will extend their life span to fifteen years or more. Always be careful when it rains, as wood decking, though it is often grooved to offer traction, can be slippery. Avoid using gravel or grass as a footing for the patio; they may perhaps be easier to install, but their upkeep is more difficult, and they do not always hold up well in all weather and with heavy use.

2

1 & 2. In a city courtyard, the absence of soil underfoot requires that plants be grown in pots and tubs, but these will allow you to easily rearrange your plants at will.

3. Wood siding with an interesting color and texture covers the house walls, enlivening this serene patio space.

2

3

4

Terraces and Decks

Functioning as extensions of the main rooms of a house, a terrace or deck in an urban setting might comprise the whole of the garden, or just a part of it. With their limited sunlight and the lack of privacy from neighbors who enjoy a bird's-eye view from upper-floor windows, ground-floor terraces share many of the same problems that face courtyards or patios, and should be approached much the same way. The higher a terrace is above the ground, the better the living conditions it can provide for plants. On rooftops, ample sun and air create an ideal environment for the cultivation of plants; and neighboring dwellings, seen as part of the overall outline of the cityscape, offer pleasant views instead of prying eyes. Plants are grown entirely in containers here, since, unlike courtyards, terraces have no ground to plant in. Planters, pots, and window boxes are the only options for your plants, which should therefore be selected for their compact habits and slow growth. Clustered together, containers allow you to grow a variety of plants in a small area, freeing up a larger space for living areas. There are some inconveniences on higher terraces and decks, though; exposure to wind and air currents creates a need for screens and trellises to use as windbreaks. These struc-

tures, which act as both decorations and supports for climbing plants, can set the tone for a modern design. These are most commonly made of wood (most often pressure-treated or naturally weather-resistant types such as redwood or teak), which is appealing because of its lightness, ease of installation, and above all, its warm look. Today, terraces are furnished like actual rooms, which can offer all the comforts of the refined life in the open air—summer kitchen, dining area, shower, solarium, and evening light. The relaxed, festive atmosphere this creates can be highlighted by the use, ever more popular in urban areas, of Mediterranean plants in terrace containers. ■

1. The proximity of a river or other substantial body of water creates a mild microclimate, allowing the cultivation of plants originally from the Mediterranean, which give the terrace an exotic flair.

2. In the city, terraces at ground level suffer from a lack of sunlight, but the sense of enclosure and seclusion they offer also gives them an intimate feeling and an atmosphere of secrecy.

3 & 4. The wood used in the flooring, the planters, and the furniture of these deck gardens creates a warm atmosphere. Specially treated wood will last longer and is easy to maintain.

Design Solutions for Difficult Environments

❁ **Surmountable inconveniences.** In an urban setting, small gardens are faced with a difficult and unwelcoming environment, hardly propitious for the cultivation of plant life. Plant acclimation and growth may be hindered by the lack of sunlight, the poor quality of the soil, and polluted air—some of the major inconveniences that those who tend these sanctuaries must cope with, along with the clamor of a noisy, overcrowded neighborhood. Fortunately, the following pages outline solutions that will make the best of all of these challenges. ■

Intrusive Neighbors

1. Small trees with a
vaselike spreading habit
combine two functions:
They shelter you from
the rays of the sun whIle
also protecting you from
inquisitive eyes.

2. A screen of small trees
arranged along the edge
of the property in an
orderly way blocks the
view from above.

.

The intrusion of prying eyes, inevitable given the proximity of surrounding buildings, is one of the inconveniences of the urban garden. However, the view from the windows of neighboring buildings, as high up as the third floor, can easily be obscured with a screen of vegetation. The simplest method consists of planting small trees that grow no higher than fifteen or twenty feet. If you use evergreens, you can have a dense obscuring screen all year long, while deciduous trees will be effective only from spring through fall. Sometimes trees arranged along the perimeter of a property can become too big and cast shade onto the center of the garden. When this ▪ ▪ ▪

• • •

happens, cut them back severely, being careful to prune them so as to keep the higher and more vertical branches; these, once filled out with leaves, will form a curtain of greenery.

Climbing plants and their supports also make an excellent means of maintaining privacy, while barely infringing on the available garden space. But here too there is an important factor to consider in using climbers to obscure the view from neighboring windows: The higher they climb, the greater the area of shade they will cast on your garden. In this case, it's best to shelter only the places where you will spend time relaxing and a few private corners, by creating screens that are more horizontal than vertical. Covering pergolas and gazebos with climbing plants will make the most of these permanent structures. Umbrellas and awnings, more ephemeral solutions, produce screens that are easy to move around, so they can be used in all different areas of the garden. ∎

1

1. Tall trees that carry their canopy of leaves high above the ground, like this golden honey locust (*Gleditsia triacanthos inermis* 'Sunburst'), free up the ground around their trunks to grow plants or to create a seating area sheltered from inquisitive eyes.

2. Vigorous and persistent, bamboo grows well in the confinement of a small city garden to form effective screens of greenery.

Harsh Climates

Climate is specific to an area. The gardens found in the Mediterranean region, for instance, are full of delicate plants that would have little chance of surviving a harsher climate. For small gardens in the city, it is important to take into account the added element of the area's microclimate. In effect, the placement of a garden in an urban milieu, the walls and buildings that surround it, and even the presence of protective trees are all elements that contribute to a unique local climate. A warmer microclimate due to the proximity of sheltering buildings, for example, may allow the cultivation of delicate species, even in a garden situated in a region with hard winters. This depends to a great extent on the course of the sun, the indispensable source of light for the growth of vegetation, and on its varying angles through the different seasons. In a small space, walls and trees make up additional obstacles that block the sun's rays. This creates shady zones whose importance can change through the year. Before you begin laying out your garden, take the time to carefully observe, over an entire year, the course of the sun, noting where it shines on the garden. It is vital to understand your garden's microclimate before you begin to arrange plantings. ∎

Tips

Trying to grow exotic, marginally hardy plants to create an original garden or establish a Mediterranean atmosphere has a great appeal to many gardeners. The environment of city gardens often lends itself perfectly to this experimentation, since they tend to have warm microclimates. You will still have to keep an eye on the drastic temperature drops in the fall and spring, and possibly protect the plants by wrapping them in burlap or row-cover fabric or bringing them into a sheltered area if the winter threatens to be a hard one.

4

3

3. In the city, a sudden hard snowfall and the cold that accompanies it risks damaging plants that are not prepared for low temperatures.

4. While garden users may appreciate the cool shade cast by surrounding buildings, it is less desirable for plants, which need sunlight to grow and thrive.

Choosing a Garden Style

Finding inspiration in the gardens of the world. The overall plan of your garden, as well as the plants and materials you choose, will all play a part in creating your garden style. It is difficult for one person to perfectly re-create the exact look and feel of a French or a Japanese garden, for cost alone if for no other reason. But if you keep in mind the architectural style of adjacent buildings, the environment of the garden, and the type of garden design you are striving for, you should have no trouble creating a unique atmosphere; the distinctive style of the garden that results can be enhanced and emphasized by the deft choice of plants and decorative elements. ■

The Zen Garden

1. Japanese gardens are one of the best sources of inspiration for small city gardens where sunlight is scarce. Replace the grass with a mosslike carpet of perennials such as Irish moss (*Sagina subulata*), baby's tears (*Soleirolia soleirolii*), or New Zealand burr (*Acaena microphylla*), and arrange a few flat stones in a line to create a stepping-stone path in a Japanese style. Adding life and movement, fine-textured grasses rise above the smooth, rounded foliage of hostas, offering a balancing contrast. Finally, to highlight the Japanese qualities of the garden, the woody plants here—loquat (*Eriobotrya japonica*), azaleas, and bamboo—are selected for their Asian origins, evergreen foliage, and graphic silhouette.

2. This Japanese-inspired garden re-creates a landscape in miniature. Interestingly eroded rocks and smooth boulders contribute to the effect, their solid, round forms harmonizing with the compact quality of the low-growing plants around them.

The Exotic Garden

1. To evoke a tropical ambience, give pride of place to shrubs and trees with architectural fans of leaves, especially those in the large family of palms. Some palms, like the windmill palm (*Trachycarpus fortunei*), which is hardy to 5°F, thrive in semi-shade.

Don't forget plants with long, sword-shaped foliage, like the cabbage palm (*Cordyline australis*) and yucca. These make for elegant combinations with the softer and more fluid grasses that suit the conditions of a small garden perfectly. Don't hesi-

tate to create dramatic contrasts by setting plants with wide, opulent, and generous leaves, like giant rhubarb (*Gunnera manicata*), next to those with narrowly dissected leaves, like fingerleaf rodgersia (*Rodgersia aesculifolia*). And remember that

nothing conveys the feeling of a jungle like a carpet of moss or a "beach" of sand and gravel.

The Potager

2 & 4. From the fall of the Roman Empire to the dawn of the Renaissance, gardens were created in farm courtyards, within the walls of manor houses, and in monastic cloisters to cultivate all of the medicinal herbs, vegetables, and fruit necessary for the residents. In these gardens, based on a simple geometrical pattern within a square, can be found the origin of the medicinal herb garden that generally adjoined a church presbytery. In our day, this style of garden is particularly well adapted to small spaces that are designed to be used both as areas of relaxation and for growing flowers, herbs, vegetables, and fruit.

3. The formal potager, outlined with boxwood borders and set off by topiary or geometrically shaped shrubs, makes a design perfectly scaled to small spaces. Pruning allows you to control the growth and volume of shrubs such as boxwood, which is the most widely used and easiest to shape. The traditional nature of these gardens should not stop you from adding a little whimsy, as here, where neatly trimmed boxwoods emerge from a more informal carpet of emerald green leaves.

2

3

4

The Romantic Garden

1 & 2. The Romantic movement, which dominated the literature and arts of the eighteenth century, had a great influence on the design of large gardens and parks. Landscape design aimed to create a veritable tableau vivant, embellished with stone sculptures or wrought-iron ornaments evoking mythological scenes and characters. Although this garden style is best adapted to grand spaces, a variation—the cottage garden—fits nicely into the closer confines of today's gardens. In the cottage garden, neatly delineated walkways and boxwood borders inject order into the artfully arranged chaos of flower beds filled with a jumble of perennials, annuals, and roses. This charming and poetic atmosphere, in which imperfections are cheerfully tolerated, encourages a spontaneous approach to gardening.

1

2

The Exuberant Garden

3, 4, 5 & 6. The exuberant garden collects more plants than it seems there is room for. Horizontal surfaces can't hold enough, so plants are suspended in baskets or trained up walls, fences, and any available structure. This type of decoration, closer to a laboratory experiment than to a garden style per se, has complete disregard for such conventions as a balanced design or a harmonious color scheme. The patchwork of colors, species, and habits that results may skate perilously close to kitschiness, but this joyous mix fosters an enchantingly naive, colorful atmosphere that is quite suited to courtyards and small gardens. To successfully pull off this riotous mosaic of foliage and flower, use mainly seasonal plants, annuals, and tender perennials, and arrange them on the ground, on windowsills, or on the tops of walls. Make full use of a variety of containers that you can move around at will. For cascading effects, hang prostrate or trailing species like million bells (*Calibrachoa*), Dahlberg daisy (*Thymophylla tenuiloba*), beggarticks (*Bidens*), fan flower (*Scaevola*), and tuberous begonias in baskets suspended with a bracket or hook from an overhang. Sit back and enjoy the show.

3

4

5

6

The Contemporary Garden

The hard-edged geometric design of the contemporary garden and the planting styles that complement it are inspired by Italian Renaissance and French gardens. Today, freed from their classical trappings, these stylish, rather formal gardens experiment with orig-

inal outlines and new materials, set off by innovative planting techniques. The contemporary garden combines tradition and modernity to accommodate our present-day style of living.

1. Here, the contemporary architecture of the house naturally calls out for a similar treatment in the garden. But even with this quite stylized organization of space, the garden remains a place to live in as well as look at. The garden's graphic rectangles do not inter-

fere with the creation of living spaces, as with the seating area adjacent to the pool.

2 & 3. Contrary to traditional styles, where the crowns of trees keep their free and fluid shapes, the contemporary garden is distinguished by its use of well-defined geometric forms, shown here in the grid of trees pruned into standards and the regular pillars of a

pergola, enshrouded with the foliage of climbing plants. In both cases, trunks and columns create a vertical link between the soil and the space above it.

4 & 5. The rhythmic repetition of tailored silhouettes and sculpted masses of vegetation offers a new take on the topiary and geometric hedges often seen in French gardens and those of the Italian Renaissance. To break with convention and strike a contemporary note while using formal topiary shapes in the garden, group them in a playful, informal way. Regular pruning allows you to control their growth and keep them in a scale well suited to a small garden. These chiseled sculptures are most original and striking when they are paired with ornamental grasses and bamboo, whose fluid, airy foliage adds a sense of light and movement.

2

3

4

5

A Design That Works

✻ **A well-thought-out plan.** Even before you begin working on your layout, make some sketches of the basic outline of the space you will have for your future garden. On a piece of graph paper re-create the space, letting each quarter-inch square represent one or two feet, depending on the size of your garden, and mark the locations of preexisting elements that you wish to or must retain, like walkways, buildings, and plants. The sketch should also distinguish between those areas to be used for plantings, those that will be left bare or as lawn, and those you wish to cover with stone, concrete, and the like. Finally, calculate how much space you have given to each of these areas, and play around with their volumes—the ratio between occupied and empty spaces. ■

1

Defining the Principal Walkways

In order to create garden prospects, you will need to create at least one path that is visible from the part of the house where you spend the most time. If the garden is square or rectangular, a diagonal path is the most effective, as it will create the longest path and therefore make the garden appear larger than it actually is.

Once these main axes have been defined, as long as you are careful not to obscure them with overgrown plants and decorative elements, they will give a sense of depth to the garden.

The field of vision should be defined at ground level with a paved or grassy surface—a pathway, for example—which will give the viewer the impression that it leads off into the distance. Garden beds on each side of this pathway, filled with more voluminous plantings, provide the mass to frame this perspective. When you stand at either end of the pathway, the entire garden will be visible to you, but it will still retain the feeling of a larger space. The pathway or avenue might be formal and straight or softly curving, depending on the style of the garden, and can taper to become more narrow at one end if need be—a trick that makes the garden look visually larger and the end of the path farther away. To close the prospect, create a concrete focal point with a decorative object or an exceptional plant at the path's end. ■

1. The longest line through this garden is the diagonal, represented by a path of flagstones surrounded by moss, which invites the eye to a distant point.

2. Starting from a terrace that serves as an extension of the house's main room, a serene grassy path follows the central axis of the garden to culminate at a decorative stone element, the focal point of a beautiful perspective.

3 & 4. To make the most of the effect of perspective, emphasize the garden's diagonal and taper off the width of the lawn to create an illusion of distance.

3

2

4

1

2

3

Creating Variations in Level

Differing levels in a garden contribute to giving an impression of space. Admittedly, they are more difficult to maintain and to travel through than a flat terrain would be, but they provide an interesting relief. Just a few steps will often be enough to create the effect of a promontory, from which there are attractive views of the rest of the garden—or even of the whole surrounding landscape.

Conversely, an area just a foot or two lower than the surrounding level of the garden can feel like a sheltered hollow, isolated from the rest of the garden. Such a sunken retreat is often welcome, especially in urban areas, for creating a sense of calm and intimacy. ■

Tips

If the terrain of your garden has natural variations in level, carefully preserve them. And if your garden is flat, there's nothing to stop you from changing the level a little. To do this, dig out an area of one hundred or so square feet, twelve to sixteen inches deep. Move the dirt you've removed to another corner of the garden to create a raised area, and plant the resulting slope with shrubs and perennials. To give access to this plateau, install a few steps and frame them with plants, decorative pottery, and garden ornaments.

1 & 4. Just a few steps are enough to give a three-dimensional feeling to a garden. The lower level, often connected to the ground floor and isolated from the rest of the garden, creates an intimate and pleasant living space.

2. A change in the level of the garden allows you to vary its ground surfaces. Here, the terrace adjacent to the house is covered with flagstones, while a deck area for relaxing, a few steps lower down, is made of wood.

3. When the ground slopes slightly, the creation of terraces linked by steps offers a succession of flat surfaces that flow down away from the house.

Defining Garden Rooms

Dividing a garden into separate spaces can be done through the use of hedges, beds of perennials or shrubs, and even trellises covered with climbing plants. The resulting succession of green alcoves or rooms can accommodate borders with different themes and diverse styles, creating a garden with many faces.

Secret garden nooks, not immediately obvious to the eye of anyone strolling through, can give the visitor the illusion of a garden that is much larger than it really is. But don't create too many of these garden cloisters, which create shady areas and risk making the garden seem fussy and cramped. Limiting the height of dividing hedges to about two-and-a-half feet allows you to create several distinct areas while still being able to look over and appreciate the whole. ■

1

1 & 2. Interrupting the space with hedges invites the visitor to linger longer. This design technique prevents the eye from immediately perceiving the limits and contents of the landscape; strollers are instead encouraged to actively seek out its secrets.

3

1

5

Working with the Surrounding Landscape

3. City gardens are usually too small to hold trees large enough to block the view from the overlooking windows, but there's nothing to prevent you from taking advantage of the greenery in neighboring properties.

4. The trees planted to provide shade along a city street can make a valuable backdrop to your garden borders, giving the impression of generous space.

5. By keeping the center of your garden free of tall plants, you create a sun-drenched open area perfect for a nice lawn or a bed of low-growing flowers.

In a small garden, too many trees of medium to large size can make it difficult to grow other shrubs and flowering plants. The conditions created by the shade of their leafy crowns and their widespread network of roots, which sap the soil of moisture and nutrients, make it virtually impossible for other shrubs to thrive under or near them. Careful observation will allow you to notice the plants just outside of your garden's perimeter. It will serve you well to take advantage of your neighbors' plantings or the curtain of leafy trees that line the street by your house by backing your flower beds up against them. By arranging plantings in this way around the perimeter of your property, and making sure to position plants so that they create a sloping bank toward the back of the border—the taller the plant, the farther back it goes in the bed—you can create a harmonious transition between your garden and its surroundings. The screen of greenery that results will also conceal the edges of your garden and make it look bigger. This arrangement leaves the center of your garden free for a sitting area, a lawn, or a bed of low-growing plants that will then have enough light to bloom. ■

Living with Large Trees

Courtyards and very small gardens cannot easily accommodate large-growing trees. If there is one already in your garden space, however, especially if it was planted decades ago and its spreading crown now masks an unsightly neighboring building, it should, of course, be carefully preserved. Large trees require regular maintenance to keep their crowns to a reasonable size for a small garden, though. A moderate pruning every two or three years will keep a tree's crown in check and allow enough light to penetrate to its feet to enable other plants to grow. Ideally, when designing your garden, choose slow-growing shrubs and trees or those that naturally reach a modest size and will not need pruning. The ever-growing number of such cultivars offered by nurserymen and landscape artists today (see the list of the best small trees in the index, page 107) is making it easier to create attractive, varied compositions in very small spaces. ∎

1

1. The great variety of forms and sizes of perennials allows you to create less massive compositions, beyond which the rest of the garden can easily be glimpsed.

2 & 3. You will not be able to fit every variety of perennial or shrub into a small garden. When selecting plants to fill your beds, then, give first priority to handsome foliage that will remain attractive throughout much of the year and has a long season of bloom.

2

Screens and Trellises

Lattice screens and decorative trompe l'oeil trellises are the most effective way to cover an old wall or a dilapidated facade. In addition, the long branches of climbing plants can be trained onto them to soften and camouflage unsightly surfaces. Simple wooden trellises latticed in squares or diamonds, painted or left natural, can produce a beautiful effect and are easy to install, either on walls or in a metal frame. But combining them with a few trompe l'oeil structures—trelliswork designs that create an illusion of depth by tricking the eye into seeing a receding perspective—can transform a space spectacularly. Placed along the axis of a walkway or at the far end of a line of perspective, these motifs can be even more effective when accompanied by decorative elements like a cast-iron wall fountain, a sculpture, a terra-cotta mask, or a mosaic of ceramic pieces to form an eye-catching focal point. Painted murals that either extend the actual plantings visually or mimic a view of a rural landscape can also push back the apparent limits of a garden. If these paintings are inserted in a trellised panel, the decorative

effect is reinforced. Even more realistic, a mirror in a wall framed by a trellis creates the perfect illusion of a garden extending into the beyond. ■

1. Interwoven osier trellises create a screen that is brought to life throughout the growing season by the foliage and flowers of twining plants, but these demand regular pruning and constant upkeep.

2 & 4. Simple trellis panels cover an unsightly wall while offering support for climbing plants.

3 & 5. In the center of trompe l'oeil trellises designed to give a false impression of depth, an architectural ornament or a mirror produce an effect both decorative and novel.

2

3

4

5

Making Your Design a Reality

❋ Now that you've spent time carefully observing your garden's environment and features, and applied the design principles laid out here for small gardens, your garden is slowly beginning to take shape. The principal axes are laid out, along with the paths and wider allées linking the areas set aside for plants. The beds are planted, screens of greenery are set in place, and the handful of pencil sketches on paper you started with begin to come to life. Even when the plan is established, however, questions are bound to remain—about the distribution of space, the impact of one bed on the overall atmosphere of the garden, or the value of a tree planted at the edge of the property. Before you move on to the stage of actually creating your garden, here are a few tips for making the best use of the smallest of spaces, creating unexpected focal points, choosing the best material to cover the ground, and above all, selecting the best plants for the garden you envision. ∎

Ornaments and Accessories

✻ **Expressing your individual style.** Plants may be the primary material in the design of a garden, but accessories, ornamental elements, and the play of water and light also add to a space's distinctive character. These elements enrich the garden's aesthetics and, above all, add an element of originality and surprise. No longer merely a gardener, the designer of the garden now takes on the role of director, whose goal is to capture the attention of visitors, drawing them in to long walks in the garden. Ideally, the garden will reveal itself little by little on these explorations, so that viewers are surprised to find that such a little space can contain such great riches. ▪

Combining Plants and Decorative Elements

1. Even the tiniest detail may make all the difference in a small garden, capturing visitors' attention, intriguing them and tempting them to linger in the garden longer. A garden that contains a number of little curiosities can create the illusion of a much larger space.

2 & 3. Topiary, clipped into imaginative tailored forms, draws the eye and lends the garden a touch of theatrical flair.

Pages 42 & 43
4 & 5 Hardly visible at first glance, unexpected ornaments and sculptures cleverly tucked away in plantings don't immediately announce themselves to visitors, but rather entice them to wander around the garden again, hoping not to miss an intriguing detail.

In the city garden, where the view of the horizon is blocked by walls and buildings, the feeling of enclosure can make a space seem much smaller than it is. As you will never be able to fit in all the ornaments and design ideas that you desire in a small city courtyard, it is important to think out your design in advance and to pay constant attention to detail. Particular care should be made in your choice of plants. The smaller the garden, the more each plant should earn its place; look especially for foliage that is attractive in color and texture and will look good through several seasons, and for flowers that are long-blooming. Another aspect to consider is how these plants will be treated—whether they will be left to their natural habit or sculpted by pruning. You can select from among plants with natural columnar, rounded, or weeping forms, as well as training or clipping specimens to create conical, square, and twisted shapes. Combining all of these profiles in an original way will make for a visually rich garden and intrigue your visitors,

distracting from the smallness of the area. Don't forget about decorative elements—sculptures, unexpected objects, garden furniture, and ornamental containers, which can contribute greatly to the overall look, completing and complementing the effects produced by trellises, trompe l'oeil screens, and mirrors. Use these to make the focal point for a distant perspective, in leafy niches, or nestled in green alcoves. However, bear in mind that if you go overboard with these ornaments, you will risk cluttering up your garden. In addition, always surround decorative elements with plants; when they are partly hidden by greenery, they will reveal themselves enticingly, bit by bit, to the stroller. You can also populate the garden with paintings or figurative sculptures to give it a feeling of life. ∎

The Play of Light

The courtyard or small garden directly connected to the house is essentially an extra room, one that profits greatly from the installation of lighting. Lighting for such a garden is first about function, illuminating spaces that are used most frequently, like seating areas and pathways. For seating areas, install ground-level spotlights, sconces attached to house walls, or light fixtures on posts that cast diffuse circles of light. Walkways should be marked out with reflectors or spotlights mounted on stakes. The more limited the space, the more important it is to illuminate recessed corners of the garden. Flower beds, garden ornaments, and even special individual plants merit being picked out with lighting. Simply set floodlights or spotlights in the ground to reveal, as night falls, the contours of forms, the texture of foliage, and the silhouettes of plants. ∎

1 & 2. Illuminating the garden allows it to be used even after night falls, as well as highlighting the silhouettes of trees dramatically. Be sure to keep the effect subtle, however, and leave a few areas dark to rest the eye and preserve a sense of mystery.

The Play of Water

There is no better way to bring a sense of life and motion to a garden or city court-yard than by furnishing it with a small pool or basin. In addition to adding a beautiful decorative object, you also create a corner teeming with life, and if you include a foun-tain, it will enhance the environment with its soothing babbling sound. The simplest way to create a water feature is to pick a pan, barrel, or aluminum tub and fill it with water. With the addition of a few small water plants to oxygenate the water, and one or two frolicking goldfish, you will have created a nearly self-sufficient ecosystem that needs little maintenance. Just keep an eye on the growth of the plants, replace the water every year, and adjust the water level regularly. To create movement, a pump will produce a murmuring stream of water that will bring a welcome sense of coolness in the summer. If the space is very small, install a wall fountain whose cascading water, fed by a closed-circuit pump, will splash down into a basin and create a melo-dious sound. If the dimensions of the gar-den permit it, a small pool created with stone or by using a pond liner will attract a

great diversity of aquatic plants and animals. In this way you can give your urban courtyard the atmosphere of an Andalusian terrace. ■

1. By reflecting a fragment of the sky, a minuscule amount of still water is enough to give another dimension to a small garden. To amplify this surprise effect and attract birds that will enjoy splashing in the water, nestle it among the ample foliage of hostas.

2 & 3. A variety of containers—here, an aluminum basin and a wooden tub—can be filled with water and find a new life as basins that can be easily moved around by their handles. The aluminum basin holds two easy-to-maintain plants: water horsetail (*Equisetum fluviatile*)

with its segmented pipelike stems, and floating watermoss (*Salvinia natans*).

4 & 5. More permanent options for water in a garden: a heavy cast-iron bird bath among hostas and a raised masonry pond against a dividing screen.

2

3

4

5

Covering the Ground

✳ **Comfort and elegance underfoot.** The flat, open areas at the heart of small gardens and courtyards, as well as those next to buildings that act as extensions to a main room of the house, are valuable spaces. They are regularly used for everyday functions or for leisure activities. A small dining area, a space for relaxation or for playing—these precious square yards must be easily accessible and comfortable to use in all kinds of weather. The choice of materials used underfoot, the way the surface is installed and maintained, and its durability thus take on a critical importance in the design of the garden. ▪

Decking

1. Wood decking is warm-looking, attractive, and lends itself to the creation of various patterns and effects. Clever manipulation of the orientation and spacing of the boards can make a garden seem larger, increasing its apparent depth or maximizing the length of a prospect.

2. When little sun is available, it is better to cover the ground with a wooden deck that allows the garden to be used in all types of weather, rather than attempting to grow a lawn

Wood is a warm, insulating, and easy-to-install material, which has led to its popularity. Tropical woods like teak, iroko, ipe, and moabi stand up well to bad weather and moisture and have a texture that is both easy on the eye and smooth to the touch. They will gradually bleach to a silvery gray unless they are treated to preserve their original color. One disadvantage of these exotic woods as a garden flooring is that they are quite pricey, due mainly to the fact that they must be shipped a long way from the warm climates where these trees grow. In addition, their popularity is leading to the destruction, in the long run, of the ecological equilibrium of the very environments that produce them. Temperate-climate species such as chestnut, acacia, fir, oak, larch, and ash do not have to be brought so far. Despite their aesthetic qualities, they have less natural resistance to humidity than the tropical woods and can be prone to rotting in damp conditions. Pressure-treated pine, in which a preservative is forced into the wood and bound in the cell wall, is quite resistant to humidity, wood-eating insects, and diseases. However, pressure-treated wood may release harmful chemicals into the environment. The relatively new process of retification is recognized as the most effective and least harmful to the environment. Used for all kinds of wood, it involves progressively heating the wood to modify its structure and to make it more dense. ■

Tips

The installation of decking is done by first building a wooden framework supported on cinder blocks or screwed into PVC bases. Many decking boards are grooved to reduce slipping after a rain. As for their maintenance, it depends on the effect that you want. If you want to maintain the original look of the wood, you will have to add a protective finish, which will need to be re-applied every two or three years. Otherwise, retified, exotic, or pressure-treated wood will lose its original color over time and fade to a silvery patina that essentially needs no maintenance.

Reconstituted Stone Slabs

Slabs of reconstituted stone are made with an agglomerate of crushed natural stone and a mortar binder. Formed into squares or rectangles, these slabs come in many styles: Some are painted with or without motifs, some have various colors of gravel incorporated, and there are even a range of slabs whose surface closely resembles that of natural stone. Colored differently according to what kind of stone is used in them, they are easy to install on a bed of sand or a slab of concrete and will acquire, in time, a lovely patina. ■

1. Reconstituted stone slabs provide many advantages, plus they are cheap and easy to install and maintain. Their look is close to natural stone and has a classic style. Here, plants grow in gaps deliberately left in the pattern of slabs, giving this garden a contemporary feel.

2

Pavers and Cobblestones

New sandstone or granite pavers are the most widely used materials for creating terraces and walkways in courtyards and small urban gardens. Their dimensions—three to eight inches wide and three to six inches high—make them easy to work with and install, and they fit well within the scale of the urban garden, as a number of small objects make a more elegant covering for the surface of a small space. Salvaged cobble stones, similar in size to new pavers, are very sought-after for their patina, which gives a look of age to the paving and a feel of authenticity to the area. In both cases, install the pavers on a bed of compacted sand or on a thin foundation of concrete. Use sand or mortar for the joints, depending on whether you wish to allow moss and grass to grow between the pavers or not. Also, make sure to create a slight slope so that water can run off after a rain. Apply a commercial algicidal treatment if the terrace is in the shade, since it may become overgrown with algae and mosses that can cause the pavers to be slippery. ■

3

2. When garden borders are arranged symmetrically around a central terrace, it is best to lay pavers of one size in a regularly repeated pattern or in neat, straight rows. This orderly effect highlights the garden's classic style.

3. Salvaged pavers of varying sizes produce a casual, irregular look that can reinforce the spontaneous style of naturalistic plantings. Arranging and setting them well can be tricky, however.

Gravel

Cheap and easy to install, pea gravel or pebbles give walkways a rustic air. Gravel should be laid over a clean, level, compact, and stable surface that has been cleared of all vegetation. To deter the invasion of weeds and to keep the soil from working its way up, you should first cover the soil with a layer of landscape fabric before spreading gravel on top. Gravel surfaces are not very comfortable to walk on because of their lack of stability, and the dust they create can be a nuisance, tracking into surrounding areas. Because of this, it is best not to place them too near the house, reserving them for more remote areas of the garden or as a temporary solution for an area that will later be covered with something more permanent. ■

1. Less muddy and dusty than bare soil, pea gravel makes a good footing near utilitarian areas. Where there is heavy foot traffic, however; soil tends to work its way up to the surface, so the gravel must be raked regularly.

2. Terra-cotta tiles installed outside produce beautiful, elegantly groomed effects and should be used for terraces close to the house. They are expensive, though, and not all types are resistant to frost.

Terra-Cotta Tiles

A noble material par excellence, terra-cotta tiles harmonize extremely well with foliage to create a warm atmosphere. Depending on the way these tiles are made—more precisely, the length of time that they are fired—some are more frost-resistant than others. Porous terra-cotta tiles allow water to penetrate, so that they are vulnerable to breakage when the water freezes and expands. This fragility limits the use of the softer handmade tiles to those regions with mild winters. It is possible, however, to find terra-cotta tiles that, by virtue of a longer firing, are durable enough to withstand all climates. Glazed tile is too slippery to use outdoors, so machine-made, high-fired, unglazed tiles are a good choice.

Set the tiles on well-tamped-down soil that has been covered with sand, and brush fine sand into the gaps between them. On a less stable surface, it is best to first lay down a light base layer of cement and set the tiles side by side into a bed of mortar, as you do when installing floor tiles in a house. In shady areas, algae and mosses can grow on the surface of terra-cotta and make it slippery. Only a power wash can remove this growth and make the terra-cotta look new again. Treating the tiles with an algicide will delay the growth of algae, but will not prevent it indefinitely. ■

1

2

Lawns

Creating a lawn in a garden that has less than a thousand square feet or so of space is not a good idea. The lack of enough sunlight, the often poor soil quality, and the competition for nutrients, space, and water from the roots of neighboring plants make this a difficult endeavor. Even when the grass does take, it will not last more than a few years; weeds and mosses will invade some areas, and foot traffic and poor conditions will create bare patches in others. In larger gardens, there may be enough sun for grass, but conditions still remain difficult, especially if the plot is encircled by trees, walls, or buildings. Low, spreading perennials or shrubby groundcovers are probably a better choice. ■

Groundcover Plantings

Perennials represent the most effective and long-lasting solution for the problem of covering the ground in a shaded garden. Varieties are available that will tolerate dense shade, constantly damp ground, and mediocre soils. Baby's tears (*Soleirolia soleirolii*), with its minuscule leaves, has the appearance of moss and will spread to cover all shaded areas. In a mild climate or an especially sheltered spot, it will retain its beautiful green foliage all year round. If baby's tears spreads too enthusiastically, which may happen if your soil is rich, mowing it or cutting it back with clippers will keep it in check. On the other hand, if there will be a lot of foot traffic over the area where it grows, it is better to create a path to walk on, since baby's tears will not wear well in those conditions. This is not the case with Irish moss (*Sagina subulata*), which tolerates fairly heavy traffic but prefers sunnier areas. If the areas you want to cover will not be walked on that often, ivy and periwinkle are appropriate species to use in shaded areas. ■

1

1 & 3. Able to tolerate the difficult conditions of a small urban garden, baby's tears (*Soleirolia soleirolii*) (1) is an excellent ground-cover to replace grass (3).

2. Ivy, which forms a beautiful green tapestry, does well in complete shade and can handle the roots of nearby trees.

2

Choosing Plants

✳ **Plants for all situations.** When choosing plants for a small urban garden, take into account their needs and the size and shape of the available plot. Every plant has specific likes and dislikes regarding climate, soil, and amount of sun, and these are often incompatible with the conditions found in cramped urban areas. It is therefore necessary to educate yourself about the nature of the soil, the hardiness zone and other factors that create the garden's microclimate, the garden's orientation to the sun, and the shade cast by buildings or trees, keeping these in mind as you begin to select plants. Eliminate at once plants that are not suited to conditions in your garden; no matter how much care you lavish on them, they are doomed to languish. ∎

Container Gardening

If you want to grow plants in a courtyard or terrace where the entire surface is paved with concrete, tile, or stone, you will need to plant them in containers. The shape and style of these containers may not affect the way the plant grows, but they will have a great impact on the style and atmosphere of your garden.

Traditional forms such as rectangular planters, window boxes, and round terra-cotta pots will blend gracefully into almost any style of garden. To make a composition more attractive, play with the size, color, and material of the containers you use. For an even more original effect, you can give almost any decorative object a second life as a planter. An interesting fruit basket or watering can discovered at a flea market can have a new life in the garden. Just be sure that there is room for enough

potting soil to give roots a place to spread and to hold an ample reserve of the nutrients and water indispensable for the growth of plants. Most plants appreciate a mix of humus and topsoil, although acid-loving plants such as azalea and others in the heath family enjoy a mix with more peat in it.

Horticultural humus, made of composted leaves and ground-up plant debris, is rich and fluffy. For containers, mix one part humus with three parts topsoil—either bought from a nursery or simply taken from the garden. After a few years, the potting mix loses its structure and becomes more like dust, at which time it is necessary to repot the plant. ∎

1. Container planting is especially effective for individual specimen plants that have exceptional form, foliage, or flowers.

2. Completely paved city courtyards force you to grow plants in containers. However, this technique allows you to change your design at any time, moving plants around at will.

3. On a terrace, a cluster of perennials grown in pots offers a valuable mass of foliage that can conceal an unsightly wall or create a temporary screen.

2

3

Beds and Borders

Most plants are happiest when planted in the ground. Even though city soil is often not of exceptional quality, it offers a volume that containers cannot rival, allowing plants to grow vigorously and attain greater size, especially valuable when you want to hide neighboring facades. The regular addition of organic soil amendments such as well-aged manure, bone meal, or garden compost will counteract the eventual loss of nutritional elements from the soil; you can easily keep track of the need for amendment with regular soil analysis. City soil can also be deficient in its makeup—overly heavy and compact in some cases, or too sandy in others. In either case, you will need to amend the soil; in the first case, incorporate sand to create better drainage, and in the second, add peat to help it retain water. The addition of good garden humus will improve both heavy and light soils. ■

1. Planting in the ground allows an extravagance of luxuriant foliage and intense color that would be impossible with container gardening.

Perennials

2. For an effective garden composition, mix ornamental grasses, colorful foliage plants, and a variety of flowering perennials. Be sure to choose plants with different bloom times to ensure an attractive display for as long as possible.

Once planted, perennials will live for several years without having to be replanted. They often develop and spread so vigorously that they need to be contained so as not to be invasive. There are a multitude of species and varieties, a good number of which are well suited to small gardens, partly because of their modest size and partly because of their ability to cope with the urban environment. You will find a list of the best of them in the index beginning on page 106. ■

Shade Plants

The vast majority of plants thrive in areas that are sunny and bright. Unfortunately, courtyards and small city gardens are often surrounded by walls and buildings that cast shade on at least part of these gardens, depriving them of the light necessary for most plants. In addition, the presence of large trees, either in the garden itself or in neighboring properties, also creates shade that, though it may be lighter, deprives plants of direct sunlight.

The shady areas common in city gardens have an impact on the choice of plants, as only those that grow in part shade will be able to flourish. A number of species of woodland perennials and ferns (see the list in the index, page 106), whose original habitat was the forest understory and glades, are very adaptable to urban conditions and offer plenty of diversity to create a variety of looks. For an elegant border, mix flowering plants with plants that have ornamental foliage. Those with striking, architectural foliage are the most appropriate when creating exuberant and exotic groupings that imitate tropical undergrowth. To give these plants the best chance to thrive, plant them in well-amended soil enriched with compost. Water them well when they are first planted, and regularly afterward, as the competition from the roots of shrubs and trees is tough. ■

1. Around this shallow basin, which has been turned into a water feature with a small fountain encircled with ivy, the finely cut emerald fronds of mossy soft shield fern (*Polystichum setiferum* 'Plumosum Densum') and autumn fern (*Dryopteris erythrosa*) contrast with the smooth chartreuse foliage of Hosta 'Gold Edger'.

2. In the shade of a Japanese maple, a dwarf bamboo, and the enormous blue leaves of *Hosta sieboldiana* 'Elegans', foamflower (*Tiarella cordifolia*) lifts its delicate stalks of white flowers.

1

Grasses

Grasses give lightness and a sense of move- ment to a composition, whether alone or with perennials or shrubs. Most grasses are deciduous, their blades glowing in fiery col- ors in the autumn before drying and fad- ing to tans and browns. Some, however, stay green throughout the winter. Easy to grow and tolerant of poor soil, the many grass species include a number that grow well in shade or full sun (see page 106). Their upkeep entails only cutting back the dead growth after the winter. To flesh out a bed or to create a novel screen, you can easily propagate grasses by dividing the clumps in the early spring. ■

1. Delicate and graceful, ornamental grasses create effective screens of foliage that sway and rustle in the wind.

1

Flowering Shrubs

This category of plant is essential in designing a small urban garden, as it creates a solid structure to build a look around. The index, page 106, lists the species and cultivars best adapted for shady areas, as well as those that need more sun. In both cases, space out the bloom times and select species that combine several attributes, such as fragrant blossoms and decorative bark in the winter or colorful foliage and attractive berries. Finally, remember that routine pruning may be necessary to encourage flowering, but proceed with caution; pruning can be particularly traumatic for shrubs that are grown in a difficult environment. ▪

2. In a small garden, reserve the sunniest spot for shrubs with flowers and colorful foliage, which need as much light as they can get to truly show themselves at their best.

1

Evergreen Shrubs

Evergreen shrubs retain their foliage throughout the winter and act as a valuable structural foundation of greenery. They can hide ugly garden walls, highlight a design, or permanently screen off an area. Above all, the presence of evergreens ensures that dismal winter weather, exacerbated by drab house walls exposed when perennials have died back, will not make the garden too gloomy. To animate a bed, set off flowering plants, and offer green relief in front of the house, a good rule of thumb is to make sure two-thirds of the shrubs you select are evergreen. The final third should be made up of deciduous shrubs that reflect the rhythm of the seasons in their emergence, full growth, autumn color, and shedding of leaves. A great number of evergreen shrubs are available in a wide variety of shades of green, which should be mixed to create a more animated picture. From the majesty of camellias to the quiet discretion of the low-growing spindle tree (*Euonymus europaeus*), from the formal solemnity of clipped boxwoods to the exuberance of bamboo, the diverse habits and sizes of these plants make them well suited to any area. See the list in the index, pages 106–7. ■

2

1. Bamboo effectively isolates a garden from its surrounding environment with a supple and graceful screen of evergreen foliage.

2. In a small space, it is best to contain the roots of bamboo, which can be particularly vigorous and invasive, by planting it in masonry containers. In the ground, it is a good idea to surround the planting hole with root-impeding landscape felt.

Tender Perennials

3. Cultivating tender plants like this New Zealand flax (*Phormium falcatum*) in containers allows them to be moved to a frost-free area when winter arrives.

Species that originate from mild or Mediterranean climates like bay laurel (*Laurus nobilis*), olives, pomegranates, or oranges, and exotic species such as palms (see page 107), are not frost-tolerant but can often be grown successfully in sheltered courtyards and small urban gardens, which may have a warmer microclimate. Here, they create a welcoming environment where visitors can imagine themselves on the Riviera or in an exotic retreat. In a harsh winter, tender specimens can be protected from frost and the wind by moving them to a veranda. Or, if there is not enough space, they can be left in place, carefully wrapped with a protective row-cover fabric. ∎

Topiary

The art of topiary, which is the clipping of shrubs to create architectural forms, began in antiquity. English boxwood (*Buxus sempervirens*), which was used extensively in gardens during the Italian Renaissance and in French gardens of the seventeenth century, is still the most commonly used species, but a number of other shrubs respond well to clipping (see the list in the index, page 107).

Topiaries are very valuable in small gardens. They occupy little space, and a specimen topiary, used as an architectural counterpoint to a more casual, naturalistic garden design, can be as effective as a sculpture in creating a strong focal point. In a different spirit, a garden composition made up entirely of topiaries in an eclectic mix of forms can produce a fantasy effect. Most often topiaries are of a clean geometric design, which is easier to create and maintain, but the most spectacular examples, representing the height of this art, spring from the idiosyncratic imaginations of their creators. Extravagant forms created in a geometric succession on the same trunk can be especially intriguing. These designs require a real mastery of the art of pruning and must be carefully and minutely clipped several times a year. Spirals or braids, and creative variations on them, also make unusual effects that show off the art of the topiary. ■

1. English boxwood (*Buxus sempervirens*) is the most common and easiest shrub to clip into geometric forms that heighten the well-manicured look of a small garden, while also adding a note of fantasy.

2. The "cloud" shapes characteristic of Japanese gardens are best formed with slow-growing species like Chinese privet (*Ligustrum delavayanum*), which demand frequent clipping.

Tips

For clipping topiaries, use special topiary shears that are kept very sharp and a wooden or iron template that, held against the plant you are shaping, will help you keep to precise lines. Clip topiaries in August or September to cut back the summer growth and again in April of the following year to cut back the growth from the previous autumn. Topiaries that represent a specific form demand considerable skill, which may take a few years to acquire. Using the wooden template to guard against slips of the shears, work in small sections, stepping back frequently to take an objective look at your progress.

1

Climbers

Climbing plants, because of their style of growth, are particularly well suited to the space of a courtyard or a small urban garden. Their canes or twining stems, which can grow several yards high, can scramble over and decorate considerable vertical areas without encroaching upon usable space at ground level. They are also very useful for ornamenting decorative structures such as pergolas, gazebos, arbors, or trellises. Virginia creeper, ivy, and climbing hydrangea use adhesive tendrils or clingy stem roots to attach themselves to vertical surfaces and therefore need no supports. On the other hand, honeysuckle, wisteria, climbing roses, and clematis all need some form of wooden or wire trellis. There are numerous species of climbing plants (see the list in the index, page 107), both evergreen and deciduous, which often form berries after flowering. Sometimes fragrant, the flowers are produced in spring, summer, or even in the middle of winter, as with winter jasmine (*Jasminum nudiflorum*). Mix several species together to combine their decorative effects. ■

1. Chinese wisteria (*Wisteria chinensis*) needs a strong support for its heavy branches, which are covered in the spring with massive mauve flower clusters.

2. Ever blooming climbing roses will lift their blossoms up on any support. You need only prune them to encourage them to rebloom and to keep them small enough to fit into your garden.

3. Climbing hydrangea (*Hydrangea petiolaris*) is one of the best climbers for small gardens, as it needs very little sun and produces elegant, creamy flower heads in the summer.

4 & 5. Virginia creeper (*Parthenocissus quinquefolia*) easily grips a wall with its clinging rootlets, smothering it with a thick carpet of foliage. A few roses or clematis cultivars planted at the base of the wall will weave themselves through the Virginia creeper, creating a beautiful effect.

2

3

4

5

Small Trees

Trees used in traditional gardens are not well suited to small urban spaces, as they rapidly become disproportionately large. Limit yourself to varieties that are naturally small and slow-growing and that will tolerate frequent pruning to control the crown, if necessary. The index (page 107) provides a list of small trees often found valuable by gardeners and available in nurseries. Give priority to standards with airy foliage that will let sunlight pass through and cast only a light shade, so they do not impede the growth of other plants underneath them. Plant them at some distance from the house, after you have determined how the shade they cast will affect the rest of the garden. It is best to plant younger specimens, as these acclimate better to transplanting. Finally, look for a combination of ornamental qualities—colorful foliage and attractive berries, for example, or elegant flowers and bark with an interesting texture. ■

1

1. Trained into a ball-like standard, the dwarf southern catalpa (*Catalpa bignonioides* 'Nana') stays naturally small and compact. Its large leaves produce a dense shade that is ideal for relaxing under, but less desirable if you want to grow other plants at its base.

2. The habit of a standard of goat willow (*Salix caprea*) brings to mind a miniature tree, perfect for the very small garden.

3. To gain the most usable space while also shielding yourself from curious eyes, high-prune a small tree so there is room to walk or sit under its crown.

2

Seasonal Plantings

Seasonal plants, whether annuals, biennials, or bulbs (see the list in the index, page 107) make good complements to the shrubs that form the backbone of the garden's design. Their color notes, which last only one season, act like punctuation marks to the overall effect. Annuals are covered in a continuous profusion of flowers from June to October. As their name implies, once they are planted in late spring, after the last frost, in pots, window boxes, or directly in the ground, they live for only one season. They are easy to grow from seed but can also be bought in the spring from nurseries as started plants in flats. There is a vast assortment; some, such as geraniums (or, more properly, pelargoniums) or fuchsia, can become perennial but are not hardy in many climates and will be killed by the first frost. To keep these plants from one year to the next, you must overwinter them in a well-lighted, well-ventilated room at no less than 40° F.

Annuals generally have decorative flowers, but some are also grown for their colorful or interestingly textured foliage. Mixed into garden beds and borders, they create a base of color and give volume to a planting.

Biennials flower from the end of winter to the end of spring, before annuals get started. They are sown in late spring or summer and planted out in the garden in late fall, just before the first frost, which they handle quite well, as they flower more generously when subjected to a cold spell.

They are called biennials because their life span straddles two years. Some, such as forget-me-nots and wallflowers, will seed themselves at the end of spring and create a pleasant surprise the following year, scattering themselves around the garden in unexpected spots.

Spring bulbs announce the coming of the warm days and can flower as early as January and as late as May. After they have flowered, their foliage should be allowed to die back naturally; the bulbs can then be left in the ground, with the exception of horticultural tulips and hyacinths, which should be dug up and stored in a cool, dry place. Plant them in autumn in mixed groups, in pots, or at the base of shrubs. Summer bulbs and tubers produce flowers from July to October and definitely need to be dug up and stored in a frost-free place over winter, as they are not cold-hardy. Among the most well known are dahlias and tuberous begonias, which often decorate pots or window boxes in the spring. ■

1. Snow-white marguerite daisies (*Chrysanthemum frutescens*) and petunias flourish in pots set out in the sun. From July to October, they are covered in flowers, especially if blooms are encouraged by deadheading.

2. Ivy-leafed geraniums produce generous cascades of flowers throughout the summer. They enjoy full sun and need little soil. In pots or window boxes, they should be given liquid fertilizer once a week and kept well watered.

3. In summer, tuberous begonias produce large, heavy flowers from tubers that have been kept in a dry, dark place throughout the winter.

4. Impatiens, often thought of as shade plants, thrive in full sun as long as they are well watered.

5 & 7. Grown in pots, window boxes, or hanging baskets, annuals come in such a variety that they can fit into any situation, bringing colorful life to every corner of the garden.

6. Impatiens have the rare quality in annuals of tolerating both shade and full sun. They bear flowers from July to October.

1

2

3

4

5

6

7

A Notebook
of Design Ideas

 Here are a few recommendations for dealing with the design problems most commonly encountered in small urban gardens. It is up to you to establish a design that suits you, once you've considered this advice. Start by setting up a schedule for creating your new garden, organized around the best times to plant—in most cases, autumn and spring. Masonry projects and any permanent structures you wish to build should generally be completed before you begin to introduce plants, so their construction does not risk damaging new beds and borders. Autumn is the best time to plant in many areas; plants benefit from the still-warm soil to develop their roots so that they can devote themselves en-

tirely to leafing out in the following spring. However, if the winter is harsh, young plants may be damaged by frost, wind, and waterlogged ground. In cold regions, therefore, it is better to plant in early spring so that the plants can take advantage of the warm summer to acclimate. Most urban spaces, protected as they are by surrounding buildings and walls, enjoy a warm microclimate that allows for planting almost any time of the year. Another reason not to wait to create the garden of your dreams. ■

A Warm Welcome

✳ **Making a successful entrance.** In the urban environment, gardens fronting the street are spaces that must be traversed to reach the house. Attention given to the style and design of these areas helps ensure an appropriate foretaste of what will be found beyond. Here more than anywhere else, the tiny dimensions of the area allow no room for error; everything can be seen at a glance. It is therefore important to make the most of an entranceway's setting through careful design and a well-considered layout of walkways and sitting areas, taking great care in the choice of both paving materials and plants. ■

The Doorway Garden

1. It is possible to entirely transform a small space into a miniature landscape—here, the layout is based around a man-made pond. When the garden must be passed through to reach the entrance of the house, however, it is best to keep the door visible so that visitors can get their bearings.

2. To simplify maintenance for a small entrance garden, just pave it entirely with flagstone. If this look is too severe and the layout too rectilinear, a few areas left unpaved and planted with shrubs or perennials will soften the harsh effect.

Even when planting a garden between the street and the house is possible in urban settings, more often than not only a very small area is available, one that must do double service as living space and space for plants. The owners of the garden will want to receive friends, relax in a pleasant setting, and devote themselves to the pleasures of gardening. An atmosphere of enjoyment should be cultivated as much as space allows. In areas dedicated to plants, you may choose to plant small trees, shrubs, and flowering plants, and sometimes even fruit trees or a small kitchen garden. The layout of these various zones should combine the useful and the pleasant, while finessing the many constraints that come with creating a garden in an urban setting. Start by laying out the path from the gate to the door. This can take the shape of a paved walkway, whose width and materials will depend on the style you are striving for, the importance of the route, and how often it will be used.

If space allows, cultivate mystery and an air of the unexpected by making the path to the front door winding, with bends that prevent the visitor from seeing the entrance of the house from all points of the garden. Let guests catch only a glimpse of the door, summoning them like a beacon. If such a layout is not possible, a clear, straight walkway to the house can be lined with several niches and alcoves created on either side for relaxation. In both cases, the area where visitors walk should be entirely covered with paving such as flagstones to make upkeep and use easy. Be aware, however, that a broad stone pathway ▪ ▪ ▪

Tips

Staging an entrance is the surest way to make a successful design. Select plants with interesting qualities, but make sure they are suited to small spaces, and decorate the garden with ornamental elements such as containers, trellises, furniture, or garden accessories. Give your entrance garden an individual character by incorporating unusual objects; utilitarian objects found in flea markets or antique shops can be converted from their original purpose to create interest and a sense of the unexpected along the path visitors travel to the door.

■ ■ ■

added to the front entrance of a stone house can result in a somewhat austere effect. As you design the layout of the entrance garden, therefore, be sure to leave areas of unpaved soil near the house and enclosing walls, or even in the middle of the paved area, where you can plant shrubs, climbers, or perennials. Spilling generously out from these planting spaces over

the paving, they will create an effect of abundance, softening the presence of the stone. ■

1. An entry full of life and texture will appear larger than it actually is. Here, the design is kept lively through the use of diverse materials in the paving underfoot, several niches of greenery, and decorative elements such as the stone trough and ceramic frog figure.

2. Garden furniture invites the visitor to pause, creating an entryway with a warm and welcoming atmosphere.

3, 4 & 5. Draw attention to a threshold or front steps by surrounding them with pottery, plants in urns or planter boxes, or sculptures. Symmetrically placed on either side, any of these ornaments will highlight the main entrance elegantly.

6 & 7. The style of the decor should match the importance of the entry. Thus, secondary entrances should be announced with simple but attractive containers, here almost hidden by foliage.

1

2

3

4

5

6

7

Furnishing the Garden

✳ **Handling garden living spaces.** In a small garden, dining nooks and areas for lounging, whether they are close to or far away from the house, can very often be seen from the house's main rooms. They therefore need particular attention when it comes to their layout and decoration. Comfortable furniture, stylish accessories, art objects, and elegant plants combine to produce a space that lures visitors out of the house. Such an inviting spot will naturally make a pleasant setting for meals, relaxation, or simply contemplation of the garden. ■

A Place to Eat

Close to the house, a garden dining area is usually an extension of the living room or kitchen. In good weather, it will be so frequently used that it becomes an extra room. To allow for easy access as well as assure visual continuity between inside and outside, which makes both spaces feel larger, it is best to keep the garden paving at the same level as the floor of the room it adjoins, and cover it with materials whose texture and color are similar, if not identical, to those of the indoor flooring. Surround a dining terrace with shrubs and flowering plants or climbers. Plants that combine several decorative attributes, such as a long and fragrant bloom time as well as colorful foliage and berries, should be selected. Consider including aromatic herbs, strawberries and tomatoes, or a grapevine: Grown in the ground or in pots, these plants strike a note of originality while at the same time providing you with an appetizing harvest from your garden. Growing plants in pots also allows you to enrich your garden palette by using plants originating from warmer climates, whose lush foliage or enticing fragrance will evoke an atmosphere of faraway, exotic lands. Container gardening makes it easier to care for these tender plants, which must be stored in a sheltered spot over winter if you wish to keep them from one year to the next.

To make your terrace a useful living space after nightfall, add some lighting to it: whether you use candles, torches, lanterns, or solar lamps, there is no shortage of choices for casting a gentle light over your dining table. To protect you from hot noonday sun, install an awning, an umbrella, or a pergola that you can cover with climbing plants. By covering part or all of the terrace, you will reinforce the intimate atmosphere of the area that makes it a valuable extension of the house.

Little sitting areas farther from the house, reached by a path through the garden, have a very different function. Even if only a few yards separate such a spot from the house, this distance can be enough to create the illusion of space. Placed to face the house or as the culmination ▪ ▪ ▪

1. Placed against the facade of the house, a dining nook directly linked to the kitchen or living room extends its space. It is easily accessible from the house, and its location allows the plantings to create a private space, screened from prying eyes and sheltered from winds. This protected location encourages the cultivation of tender plants native to warmer climates, which give this nook an exotic atmosphere of faraway lands.

2 & 3. Little sitting niches surrounded by flourishing greenery offer beautiful views of the house and the garden. Too far from the amenities of the kitchen to be easily used for a full-scale dinner, they are better adapted to casual snacks and picnics. They are visible from the main rooms of the house, though, so make sure to choose furniture that matches the style of the garden and harmonizes with its overall look. Metal furniture, for example, is durable, but it may be a bit uncomfortable unless it is equipped with seat cushions.

2

3

of a garden pathway, these spaces at a distance from the house allow the visitor to sit back and take in the whole view. Whether your dining patio is against the house or set apart, make sure the paved area is stable enough to hold a nice table and spacious enough that everyone can sit comfortably. Plan for enough room to accommodate a large number of guests, and be sure that you choose an area that gets good sunlight throughout the year and is sheltered from winds. ■

1

1. Placed in the center of a garden and surrounded by greenery, this dining area has the benefit of a lot of sunlight and a pleasant environment, but is open to everyone's view.

2. A deep roof overhang draped generously with vegetation assures effective protection from the sun, the rain, and curious eyes, but considerably darkens the adjacent rooms.

3. A pergola with a translucent cover, an awning, or a glass roof provides protection from the rain while still letting light through, thus allowing it to be filled with plants.

2

2

3

4

5

1. To choose the best place for a dinner nook, observe the daily course of the sun at different times of the year to determine the shade cast by buildings and plants. If space allows, find two alternate spots; while the sun may be appreciated in the spring and autumn, it will be less desirable in the summer, when shade is more

welcomed. Make sure the dimensions of the furniture are in scale with the dining area.

2. In a small garden, opt for round café-style tables and small-scale chairs. It is also best to use a delicate, airy style, such as wrought iron, which can be discreetly integrated into the decor and sets off greenery

nicely. Choose colors to match your intended look. Dark colors close to the green of foliage blend into the background more easily than light shades.

3. A dinner nook situated directly off a living room acquires the stature of an extra room, given its proximity to the house and the use of furniture

and interior accessories. This agreeable way to use garden space is only possible if the patio is protected by over-hanging eaves or a glass roof. You can also push out the limits of the dining room in a similar way by installing an outdoor kitchen with a working counter on an adjacent patio.

4 & 5. In an urban setting, large umbrellas are indispensable not only for protection from the sun but also, and perhaps more important, from onlookers in surrounding buildings. Dark colors cast a deeper shade that reinforces the intimacy of the area, but can come across as too somber. Light colors produce a brighter

atmosphere, but get dirty quickly and need frequent cleaning.

A Place to Relax

Lazing about in the garden, immersed in contemplation of its emerald shades, is one of the gardener's favorite activities. She will take advantage of these quiet moments to congratulate herself on work well done, observe the fauna and flora, or meditate on future designs or projects. Even the smallest of gardens should make room for a place to retreat from busy throughways, furnished with a bench or at the very least a comfortable chair. Choose a spot that is protected from the eyes of others but also offers a broad view over the garden—backed up against a wall, a hedge, or a trellis covered with twining vines. Cover the ground with a few flagstones or pavers, not only to keep mud at bay but to differentiate this spot from the surrounding area. Link it to the rest of the garden with a discrete path that will allow you to reach it at all times of the year without getting your feet wet. Surround it with greenery to create an alcove that reinforces the feeling of intimacy, and find a comfortable bench, made with material that is easy to take care of and dries quickly after showers. After all, it is precisely those times, just after a rain or after watering the garden, when the ground and the leaves of plants are emitting their most seductive fragrances, that we most value this privileged point of observation.

As with a dining area, carefully choose plants that add to the air of serenity. Select perennials and flowering shrubs with evergreen foliage, to create a screen of greenery throughout the year. Add a romantic touch with an arch or pergola covered with climbing plants such as roses, honeysuckle, jasmine, or clematis, which produce garlands of flowers and cascades of foliage. You can add some background sounds to this charming picture by installing a basin with a simple jet of water, a fountain, or even bird feeders, so you can enjoy the chirping of feathered visitors. ∎

1 & 2. Hidden in greenery, a relaxation space is a pleasant and calm place that should be kept well manicured, especially in a small garden where it is often well in view from the main rooms of the house.

3. Although almost hidden by a luxurious cascade of leaves, a garden retreat can be a showpiece that attracts guests into the garden. Here, a classically shaped bench painted deep blue is set off by the golden foliage of hops.

1

2

Screens and Concealment

✻ **The art of camouflage.** In a small garden, everything is visible, and the slightest imperfections lie blatantly open to the eyes of both visitors and the garden's owners. The latter, however, end up noticing these faults less and less as, little by little, they simply become part of the decor. This is why, when first creating a garden, you must stick to your plan right through to the end, paying attention to the smallest detail; anything you put off until tomorrow will probably never get done. ■

Softening a Facade

In a small garden, vertical surfaces are the most visible structures. The vertical facades of buildings, houses, or enclosing or dividing walls become more imposing the smaller the garden area is.

The wall of a house is perhaps the most visible surface, but is also without a doubt the easiest to relieve and enliven. Doors and windows interrupt the uniformity of this wall and give it a certain rhythm. Covering the walls of buildings that have recently been restored, repainted, or had new siding installed will not be as necessary. However, asymmetrical openings, deteriorated brick or siding, flaking paint, or unsightly gutters, vents, or downspouts can be enough to mar a wall's aesthetics.

To cover up these defects without intruding on usable garden space, use climbing plants that take up little room on the ground. On their own, these can weave a curtain of foliage or garlands of flowers over an unsightly wall. Some, like ivy or climbing hydrangea, can cling to most surfaces with small tendrils or rootlets (though these can damage the surface of the wall). Others need a support to help them climb,

as is the case with climbing roses, clematis, and honeysuckle, whose canes must be trained along a trellis or wire. These decorative structures can help to dress up the area and can hold the branches of other plants. Ornamental shrubs—camellias, California lilac (*Ceanothus* species), or firethorn (*Pyracantha*)—are easily trained onto a support, where they produce an original effect by transforming a facade into a wall of flowers, foliage, or colorful berries. Whatever you use, be sure to keep growth in check with regular pruning, taking special care that climbers do not overwhelm windows and darken the rooms of the house. Cover the plants' often bare lower stems with a border of perennials or small shrubs. ■

1. To conceal an awkward asymmetrical arrangement of windows or camouflage the imperfections of a facade, use climbing plants and ornamental shrubs. However, don't let the plants encroach upon the windows and risk darkening the house. Also, keep them well trimmed close against the edifice with regular hard pruning. Hide the base of climbing plants with a bed of perennials.

2. Using climbing plants along a facade does not always mean completely hiding the entire surface of a wall or house. Here, some carefully trained branches of Virginia creeper create horizontal ribbons of foliage, breaking up a monotonous blank wall.

3. A wooden trellis helps give climbing plants a foothold so they can decorate a facade. It also effectively hides utilitarian structures like drainpipes without making them inaccessible.

2

3

Disguising a Wall

Enclosing walls are a fact of life in small urban gardens, as they are the only effective means of isolating your garden from neighbors' views and noise. On the other hand, they can be sheer and austere surfaces that you may want to cover or conceal. Wood, natural stone, and carefully laid brick facings are attractive enough that they do not need to be covered. Those made of cinder blocks or thickly mortared brickwork, though, are best covered up with plaster or stucco, whose color will influence the feeling of space. To lessen the depth or size of a space, for example, choose light colors, such as white, ocher, or beige, which will set off both plants and ornamental objects clearly. (You will have to evaluate just how much contrast you want between the wall and the plants.) Dark colors such as deep red, brown, or green, tend to merge into the background shade, making the wall more difficult to see. This will make it harder to tell the precise location of the wall, and consequently the entire space may seem bigger than it actually is. The color should also match the atmosphere you are trying to establish in the garden.

Vibrant colors such as red and yellow are tonics, invigorating and cheering in their effect; greens and blues are more calming; and orange evokes the sun and warmth. Just as for the facade of a house, it is also possible to conceal or soften a wall by covering it with trellises or greenery. Climbing plants, ornamental shrubs, and perennials—with the diversity of their habits, the varied texture and hue of their foliage, and the numerous colors of their blossoms—can raise a stark, somber, vertical surface to the rank of an indispensable backdrop. ■

2

1. In beds along the foot of a wall, as well as with climbers higher up, using plants with a diverse range of habits and leaf and flower colors will attract attention to the garden composition and away from the structure itself.

2. In small courtyards and urban gardens, the absence of soil makes it necessary to garden in containers. To successfully grow shrubs and climbing plants, such as hydrangeas and winter-flowering clematis (*Clematis armandii*), use tubs that are at least twenty inches deep. In spaces that receive little sunlight, shade-tolerant plants such as skimmias, Japanese pieris (*Pieris japonica*), azaleas, or rhododendrons can also be grown in pots.

3. Make the most of the space in a small urban garden or courtyard by growing climbing plants up the surrounding walls, instead of planting shrubs, which will billow out and encroach upon living areas. At the far end of this small courtyard, the terrace is raised a few steps, and a curtain of greenery is kept close against the walls to minimize the feeling of enclosure they create.

4 & 5. In small courtyard gardens that are entirely paved, walls can be livened up with planters and hanging baskets, which create a charming patchwork of colors and materials. Against a backdrop of ferns or pruned boxwoods, tuberous begonias, geraniums, and impatiens create a symphony on one theme: the color white. This shade, at once neutral and luminous, exemplifies elegance in a garden.

3

4

5

Fences and Screens

Boundary fences and walls must be opaque if they are going to truly protect your garden from wind and the eyes of neighbors. They are thus usually made of wood, natural or man-made stone, or concrete. Combined with building walls and facades, however, these solid materials tend to heighten the feeling of confinement. To lessen this effect, begin by getting in contact with your neighbors, who will, of course, want to find a solution that keeps everyone on good terms. Together, you can work out a plan for a dividing wall that alternates between solid sections for privacy, and open segments to offer a glimpse of more distant views. Fences made of wood boards, in addition to their warm and natural look, offer a number of design possibilities and can serve as elegant supports for climbers, the category of plants most suitable for ornamenting such structures. Together you should also decide on one or two larger shrubs or trees whose branches will spread out over both sides of the dividing wall; because less space will be devoted to their spreading roots, you can grow a number of smaller plants along the divider. To add a festive note, hang baskets of trailing annuals from the top of the divider at regular intervals. ■

1. To conceal the top of a fence or wall, use climbers or trailing annuals such as tuberous begonias, 'Surfinia' petunias, million bells (*Calibrachoa*), or ivy-leaf geraniums.

1

Tips

In very small urban gardens, consider taking advantage of the greenery of neighboring gardens by reducing the height of your fences or leaving gaps in a dividing wall. Shorter fences will create a feeling of depth and make your own garden seem larger. Keep a solid dividing wall near the house, close to the main traffic routes and living areas. You can leave occasional gaps in dividers to accommodate trees or a trellis covered with climbing plants.

Retaining Walls

2. Softening the effect of this retaining wall, upright perennials like artemisia and woodland sage (*Salvia nemorosa*) rise from its base, and trailers like fleabane (*Erigeron karvinskianus*) and boxleaf hebe (*Hebe buxifolia*) cascade down from its top.

Small differences in the height of the terrain usually require a low wall that will be connected to other walls and facades. To better integrate these retaining walls into your garden design, use natural materials like wood or stone and help them to blend in by letting the foliage of ground-hugging shrubs and rock-garden perennials soften their edges. Planted along the top of a low wall, these plants will spill over the side of the wall, almost obscuring its face. To complete the effect, you can leave a narrow band of soil beneath the wall, and fill it with plants whose foliage and flowers will rise to screen it from below. ■

Neighboring Buildings

1 & 2. Hedges and small trees planted along the boundary between two city gardens should not be higher than six feet, which is insufficient to block the view from overlooking structures. In very small spaces, an umbrella is the only way to assure privacy.

3. Pergolas, gazebos, and trellises covered with climbing plants provide a natural and effective vegetative screen between a living area and neighbors, but they block the sun's rays.

4. Planting a tree is one solution for larger gardens. Choose a species with airy foliage, and high-prune it to allow for more room under and around it, and for sunlight to shine through.

A small garden is a haven of greenery that attracts the fascinated attention of others, especially when it is found in the very heart of a city. This makes it difficult to putter around in it without feeling spied upon. Hiding from the inquisitive eyes of neighbors at windows above or of passersby on the street is one of the principal preoccupations of the owners of urban gardens. Begin by determining the view from surrounding areas, at different levels, onto the parts of the garden where you'll be spending time. Then evaluate the impact of solutions such as planting small trees or installing trellises covered with climbing plants. To aid you in judging how effectively these protective structures will block neighbors' view, run a few trials by setting up temporary posts where you intend to put them. A well-placed plant or a short section of trellis may be enough to shield a corner of a terrace without blocking too much sun or making you feel hemmed in.

In a very small garden, it is impossible to plant trees and to build long stretches of trellis. To afford shelter from neighbors in these conditions, there is no other solution than to use an umbrella or construct a pergola over the terrace or sitting area. More spacious gardens can accommodate a line of trees, kept regularly pruned into a narrow screen, around their borders. ∎

1

2

3

Making the Most of Awkward Features

Converting unsightly areas into beautiful settings. In a small garden or courtyard, or on a terrace on the same level as the rest of the garden, there is always an awkward spot that is not only inconvenient, but too often visible from the main rooms of the house. Steep banks, shady areas, or places under trees where nothing can compete with the roots are situations that are encountered all too often. Here are a few valuable suggestions for transforming these ugly patches into elegant features. ■

Steep Slopes

Terraced banks are a way to cope with a large difference in levels in the garden. They are indispensable when the basement of a house is accessible from the garden or when the ground floor is raised. The sloping bank gives relief and interest to the garden, but it is difficult to develop and very complicated to maintain. As it also effectively makes it impossible to have a grass lawn, which would be too difficult to mow, a steep bank encourages a design inspired by alpine rock gardens, combining perennials and low-growing shrubs. Begin by stabilizing the ground with a retaining wall of landscape timbers, railroad ties, brick, or natural stone. Then select plants adapted to such soil with varying heights and plant forms, harmonizing the hues of the foliage and the flowers. For sunny areas, choose rock garden perennials with low, spreading or cushion-forming habits. Keep bloom time in mind, using plants whose seasons of bloom overlap to prolong the display, evergreen species like conifers and dwarf shrubs provide a valuable backdrop to seasonal bloomers. For shady areas, choose among the ferns, grasses, and perennials found naturally in woodland understories. ■

2

1 & 2. An embankment that bridges the difference in level between the garden and a raised ground floor can make an effective stage setting against the house, highlighting plantings by lifting them up closer to eye level. This is a good opportunity to play with plant heights and foliage color and texture to create a lively tableau.

3. The drop in level from the garden to a basement entrance is accommodated by low stone retaining walls, softened by a tapestry of ground-hugging rock plants.

3

Shady Corners

1 & 2. Balancing design and nature, these two gardens make the most of a shady setting. The first plays carefully pruned boxwoods and spindle trees (*Euonymus europaeus*) against each other to compose an ensemble of volume and geometric form. The other contains the fluid silhouettes of grasses inside low borders of the groundcover barren strawberry (*Waldsteinia ternata*).

Making shade your ally is essential in an urban garden, surrounded as it is by buildings, walls, and hedges. The shade cast by barriers of stone or vegetation is so intrinsic to these spaces that it is best to design with it in mind. First, locate the garden's sunniest spot, which is a good place to put a table and chairs, so you can take advantage of a bit of sun. Take the time to observe the course of the sun over an entire year so you can precisely locate this area. Since this will not necessarily be the same in every season, you may want to set up several little seating areas, taking advantage of one sunny corner in the winter and another in the summer. Then organize the garden into areas according to their use—places to sit and relax or dining areas, for

example—and create beds of plants that tolerate shade around them. The most suitable shrubs and perennials will be those whose natural habitat is the forest understory. Plants with light green foliage are best, so as not to make a shady area even darker. Balance the form and style of shrubs, mixing those with a loose, informal habit with more geometric clipped shapes, whose contours will be highlighted by the effect of light and shade. In shady areas, use light, warm colors like ochers, yellows, and oranges on wall surfaces, on the ground, in your choice of flowering plants—even in chair cushions and accessories. These bright hues will bring a touch of sun and warmth into the gloomiest corner. ■

Under Trees

In existing gardens—as with those created around new construction—trees are worth preserving and integrating into future designs for the shade they offer during the summer, for the value of their foliage as a green backdrop, and for the protection they afford from nosy neighbors. Many are remarkable in their size or their habit and must be protected out of respect for their venerable age and beauty. A tree species can also have a botanical value if it is rare or reputed to be difficult to grow in the region. Beyond these concerns, the presence of a venerable tree testifies to the respect that the bygone owners of the place had for it. The tree's history is often intertwined with that of the gardener who, in his passion for the plant world, expended all of his energy in the cultivation and care of the tree. For all of these reasons, do not rashly cut down a tree in haste; take the time to live with it over a few months, perhaps even a few years, in the garden. During this time, pay attention to the shade it casts as the sun moves across the sky daily and through the seasons, and study its impact on the space. Then plan a campaign of pruning to lighten the crown, and cut away low branches so that you may add plantings around its base. In full shade, only ivy and periwinkle (*Vinca minor*) can grow, which is a very limited choice, but you can add spring bulbs that will bloom in the sun that gets through before the tree leafs out to create denser shade. In partial shade, your options are wider and include many perennials and ferns whose native habitat is the dappled shade of the forest understory. ■

1. To illuminate a garden shaded by a venerable or remarkable tree, high-prune the tree, removing lower branches. Thinning the crown will allow more sun through without changing the overall shape of the tree. On the ground, only ivy will thrive in this environment. It produces an elegant and uniform carpet of emerald green, which can be embellished in spring with a few colonies of narcissus.

2. The layout of this small garden is adapted to the presence of a centenarian tree. Hostas, oak-leaved hydrangea (*Hydrangea quercifolia*), goatsbeard (*Aruncus dioicus*), and ferns spread from the base of its trunk to grace the edge of a pool. Such a design requires that dead leaves be removed from the pool regularly.

3. At the foot of a tree, intrusive roots make it necessary to create a slightly raised bed to assure enough soil for other plants, such as Irish ivy (*Hedera hibernica*).

1

2

Indexes

Index of the Best Plants for City Gardens

Leucothoe cultivars

Oleaster, *Elaeagnus x ebbingei*

Osmanthus burkwoodii

Portugal laurel, *Prunus lusitanica*

Privet, *Ligustrum* species

Privet honeysuckle, *Lonicera pileata*

Red-tipped photinia, *Photinia x fraseri*

Rhododendron cultivars

Southern magnolia, *Magnolia grandiflora*

Spindle tree, *Euonymus* species

Evergreen Shrubs for Full Sun

English lavender, *Lavandula angustifolia*

Escallonia cultivars

Holly tea olive, *Osmanthus heterophyllus*

Jerusalem sage, *Phlomis fruticosa*

Rosemary, *Rosmarinus officinalis*

Russian sage, *Perovskia atriplicifolia*

Tree mallow, *Lavatera* cultivars

Tender Shrubs

Bay laurel, *Laurus nobilis*

Bougainvillea cultivars

Canary Island date palm, *Phoenix canariensis*

Cape leadwort, *Plumbago auriculata*

Cider gum, *Eucalyptus gunnii*

Convolvulus species

Crape myrtle, *Lagerstroemia* cultivars

European fan palm, *Chamaerops humilis*

Italian cypress, *Cupressus sempervirens*

Lavender cotton, *Santolina chamaecyparissus*

New Zealand flax, *Phormium* species

Oleander, *Nerium oleander*

Passionflower, *Passiflora caerulea*

Pittosporum tobira and *P. angustifolium*

Senecio greyii

Strawberry tea, *Arbutus unedo*

Shrubs for Topiary

Arizona cypress, *Cupressus arizonica*

Boxwood, *Buxus* species

Box honeysuckle, *Lonicera nitida*

Laurastinus, *Viburnum tinus*

Leyland cypress, *Cupressocyparis leylandii*

Myrtle, *Myrtus communis*

Port Orford cedar, *Chamaecyparis lawsoniana*

Privet, *Ligustrum delavayanum* and *L. ionandrum*

Privet honeysuckle, *Lonicera pileata*

Yew, *Taxus baccata*

Climbing Plants for Full Shade

Clematis montana

Climbing hydrangea, *Hydrangea petiolaris*

Dutchman's pipe, *Aristolochia durior*

Ivy, *Hedera helix*

Silver lace vine, *Polygonum aubertii*

Climbing Plants for Full Sun

Clematis hybrids

Confederate jasmine, *Trachelospermum jasminoides*

Grape, *Vitis vinifera*

Honeysuckle, *Lonicera* species

Jasmine, *Jasminum officinale*

Trumpet creeper, *Campsis* cultivars

Virginia creeper, *Parthenocissus* species

Wisteria species

Small Trees

Amur cherry, *Prunus maackii*

Amur maple, *Acer ginnala*

Antarctic beech, *Nothofagus antarctica*

Dwarf Scotch pine, *Pinus sylvestris* 'Nana'

Dwarf southern catalpa, *Catalpa bignonioides* 'Nana'

Eastern hemlock, *Tsuga canadensis*

Field maple, *Acer campestre*

Globe Norway maple, *Acer platanoides* 'Globosum'

Goldenrain tree, *Koelreuteria paniculata*

Honey locust, *Gleditsia triacanthos inermis* 'Sunburst'

Japanese maple, *Acer palmatum*

Paperbark cherry, *Prunus serrula*

Persian ironwood, *Parrotia persica*

Silk tree, *Albizia julibrissin*

Snakebark maple, *Acer davidii*

Umbrella black locust, *Robinia pseudoacacia* 'Umbraculifera'

Weeping willowleaf pear, *Pyrus salicifolius* 'Pendula'

White mulberry, *Morus alba*

Annuals and Nonhardy Plants for Summer

African daisy, *Osteospermum* hybrids

Beggarticks, *Bidens ferulifolia*

Blue marguerite, *Felicia amelloides*

Edging lobelia, *Lobelia erinus*

Euryops 'Sunshine'

Fan flower, *Scaevola*

Fleabane, *Erigeron karvinskianus*

Flossflower, *Ageratum* 'Blue Ball'

Flowering tobacco, *Nicotiana* cultivars

Fuchsia hybrids

Gaura lindheimeri

Gazania pinnata

Heliotrope, *Heliotropium* species

Impatiens cultivars

Ivy-leafed and zonal geraniums, *Pelargonium* cultivars

Leadwort, *Plumbago*

Marguerite daisy, *Chrysanthemum frutescens*

Marigold, *Tagetes* cultivars

Moss rose, *Portulaca* hybrids

Nasturtium, *Tropaeolum* cultivars

Ornamental sage, *Salvia* cultivars

Petunia hybrids

Sanvitalia procumbens

Slipperwort, *Calceolaria rugosa*

Swan River daisy, *Brachycome iberidifolia*

Sweet alyssum, *Alyssum* hybrids

Verbena cultivars

Yellow sage, *Lantana camara*

Plants with Colorful Foliage

Beef plant, *Iresine herbstii*

Coleus cultivars

Flowering maple, *Abutilon*

Lavender cotton, *Santolina chamaecyparissus*

Licorice plant, *Helichrysum petiolare*

Swedish ivy, *Plectranthus coleoides* 'Variegatus'

Biennials

Bellflower, *Campanula media*

Cottage pink, *Dianthus plumarius*

English daisy, *Bellis perennis*

Forget-me-not, *Myosotis* hybrids

Viola hybrids

Wallflower, *Cheiranthus cheiri*

Bulbs for Spring

Crocus hybrids

Cyclamen coum

Daffodil, *Narcissus pseudonarcissus*

Grape hyacinth, *Muscari* species

Hyacinth, *Hyacinthus*

Italian bluebell, *Hyacinthoides italica*

Lily-of-the-valley, *Convallaria majalis*

Snowdrop, *Galanthus nivalis*

Tulip, *Tulipa* hybrids and species

Wood anemone, *Anemone blanda* and *A. nemorosa*

Bulbs for Summer

Asiatic and Oriental lilies, *Lilium* species

Canna hybrids

Dahlia hybrids

Tuberous begonia, *Begonia tuberhybrida*

General Index

Acknowledgments

The authors, Pierre Nessmann and Brigitte and Philippe Perdereau, would like to kindly thank the owners, gardeners, and designers who opened the gates to their gardens and their creations.

Front cover: Garden design by Kristoff Swinnen, Saint-Nicolas, Belgium
Back cover: top left, garden design by Arend Jan Van Der Horst; top and bottom right, garden design by Kristoff Swinnen; bottom left, garden design by Erwan Tymen

Garden design by Erik Borja: 76
Garden design by Callarec-Le Carvennec: 40
Glen Chantry garden: 62
Garden design by Chevalier-Frinault, 29 bottom left, 80, 95, 96 top left and bottom left, 97, 99 top
Clos du Chemin garden: 37 bottom
Garden design by Didier Danet: 52 right, 57 left
Garden design by Dira Deferme: 24 top, 32 top, 47 bottom left, 89 left
Garden design by Guilmain Dinard: 35, 74, 86 right
Garden design by Pascal Garbe: 13, 42
Garden design by Chrys Ghyselen: 64 top, 83
Guell garden: 37 top, 99
Paradis garden: 87
Garden design by Nathalie Payens: 22
Pays d'Auge garden: 81
Petite Chabotte garden: 9 left, 10 bottom
Garden design by Hugues Peuvergne: 52 left
Plantbessin garden: 23 bottom
Retz garden: 86 left, 88, 90
Garden design by Pierre-Alexandre Risser: 8, 14, 47 top left, 67, 68, 79 top right
s'Gravenswesel garden: 100
Garden design by Kristoff Swinnen: 11, 26, 27 top left, 44–45
Garden design by Erwan Tymen: 17, 18 top, 22 bottom, 27 bottom left, 27 right, 30, 32 bottom, 34 bottom, 36, 41 right, 48–49, 50, 51 bottom, 53, 61, 63, 77, 78, 79 bottom left, 85 top left, 85 bottom right
Garden design by Arend Jan Van Der Horst: 27 top right, 85 bottom left
Garden design by Timothy Vaughan: 31, 51 top, 82
Verhayen garden: 56, 60, 65, 73 bottom left, 92, 93 bottom left, 93 bottom right
Garden design by André van Wassenhove: 4–5, 16, 101
Garden design by Jacques Wirtz: 56